IT IS TIME TO MEET

St. Philomena

It Is Time to Meet

St. Philomena

Mark Miravalle

QUEENSHIP PUBLISHING COMPANY

Queenship Publishing Company
P.O. Box 220
Goleta, CA 93116
(800) 647-9882, (805) 692-0043, Fax: (805) 967-5843
www,queenship.org

Printed in the United States of America

Library of Congress Number #2007928463
ISBN: 978-1-57918-333-6

DEDICATION

To our daughters
Sr. Maria, Mariana,
Annaleah, Mary-Bernadette,
Philumena

CONTENTS

INTRODUCTION

I would like to introduce you to a young, early virgin-martyr, who has received extraordinary honor in the Church from popes, bishops, saints, and mystics. Pope Gregory XVI referred to her as the "wonder-worker" of the nineteenth century. Bl. Pope Pius IX declared her the "Patroness of the Children of Mary." St. John Vianney attributed all of his miracles to her, stating, "I have never asked for anything through the intercession of my Little Saint without having been answered." Bl. Anna Maria Taigi, the Roman "mother-mystic," received through this saint the miraculous cure of her granddaughter, and entrusted all her children to her powerful intercession. And the popes of the nineteenth century showered this young saint with numerous plenary indulgences, and gifts such as papal rings and pectoral crosses.

It is time for you to meet St. Philomena, "Powerful with God," in the words of Gregory XVI. As she was a "thaumaturga" of the nineteenth century, so she continues her wonder-working ways in our twenty-first century. Devotion to St. Philomena is spreading like a re-kindled wildfire throughout the universal Church today, with testimonies to her miraculous intercession being received by the international shrine of St. Philomena in Mugnano, Italy, from all parts of the world. St. Philomena wishes to exercise her remarkable power of intercession, precisely for you.

CHAPTER I

THE DISCOVERY OF
ST. PHILOMENA

On May 24, 1802, workers digging in the ancient Catacombs of Priscilla in Rome made an exciting discovery. While excavating near the "Greek chapel," one of the earliest sections of the catacombs, they found a previously unrecorded grave, a type of grave hewn out of the rock called a *loculus*. Sensing the importance of what they had unearthed, and following the instruction given them by Msgr. Hyacinth Ponzetti, the Vatican Custodian of Holy Relics, work was immediately halted and Fr. Filippo Ludovici, the official Vatican overseer of all excavations, was informed.

The next day, May 25, 1802, Fr. Ludovici entered the catacombs with several other observers and officially documented the new grave. It was found to be sealed by three terra-cotta brick tiles arranged side by side. Engraved on the tiles were a palm branch, typically used to symbolize martyrdom, arrows, a lily, typically used to symbolize purity or virginity, and an anchor. On the tiles, painted in red from left to right was an inscription: the first tile read "LUMENA," the second tile "PAXTE," and the third read "CUMFI." An anatomical examination of the bones found within led to the conclusion that the person entombed was a young girl approximately twelve to thirteen years old. Also found in the grave was a vial of dried blood, which was the early Church's typical manner of indicating the grave of a martyr.

Msgr. Ponzetti, the Vatican custodian of holy relics, read the tiles according to the ancient custom of starting with the second tile, as "PAX TECUM FILUMENA," or "Peace be with you, Filumena," and officially rendered the young martyr's name as "Filumena" (Philomena in English). Msgr. Ponzetti sought historical records for "Filumena" but none were found.

Not long after the discovery of the tomb, a humble parish priest, Fr. Francesco di Lucia from the small town of Mugnano near Naples, arrived in Rome seeking relics of a martyr to spiritually re-vitalize his parish which had grown "weak in virtue," according to the pastor. Through the special assistance of di Lucia's bishop-elect of Nola, Msgr. Bartolomeo de Caesare, wherein Mugnano was located, in 1805 Pope Pius VII consigned the sacred remains of "Filumena" to Fr. di Lucia for the people of Mugnano.

Fr. di Lucia took the relics from Rome back to Mugnano, and the ride home turned out to be rather unusual. At one point, the priest heard a knocking that came from the box containing the sacred remains of Filumena. As the knocking continued, Fr. di Lucia realized that the sacred remains were underneath the carriage, which was not a particularly reverent location for sacred relics. He decided that these holy remains should ride next to him in the carriage, and when they were put in this more reverential place, the knocking ceased for the remainder of the journey.

When Fr. di Lucia stopped over in Naples at the home of the Terrès family, there began the miracles of healing for which St. Philomena was soon to become famous.

The Porter who assisted in carrying the virgin-martyr's relics was instantly cured of nephritis, and a lawyer with severe sciatica who was carried into the family chapel was instantly cured.

A woman present who had a cancerous ulcer, and who was scheduled for amputation the next day, was also instantly cured of both cancer and the spreading gangrene when a relic of St. Philomena was placed over her sores.[1]

Immediately upon the arrival of the remains of Philomena in Mugnano on August 10, 1805, bishops and parish priests of the region began to officially document an extraordinary number of miracles. Here are just a few examples as recorded in the diocesan and parish archives, and later submitted to the Holy See.

As soon as the sacred body of Philomena entered Our Lady of Grace parish church, the church bells starting ringing on their own. The town paralytic, Angelo Bianco, upon merely hearing the bells was instantly cured and ran into the church—to the amazement of all in attendance.

Within the first week of the arrival of "Filumena," a mother of a blind son dipped her fingers into the oil of the lamp burning beside the tomb, placed the oil on the eyes of her son, and he was instantly healed.[2]

This constituted only the first week of the miraculous intercession of Philomena, all officially documented in the archives of Our Lady of Grace church in Mugnano, and confirmed by the local Bishop of Nola.[3]

Over the next few years, the fame of Philomena spread throughout Italy and beyond. There were numerous reports of miracles, and many of these reports reached Pope Gregory XVI.

For example, the renowned Roman mystic, Bl. Anna Maria Taigi, prayed daily to Philomena. When her granddaughter, Peppina, seriously damaged her eye by tearing the pupil irreparably, Bl. Anna Maria blessed the child with some oil of Philomena, which had come from the lamp burning next to her tomb. The next morning Peppina had perfect sight, and the miracle was confirmed by several doctors' examinations. On her deathbed, Bl. Anna Maria entrusted her family and children to Philomena's care.[4]

When the Holy See began to consider elevating the devotional status of Philomena to the altar of the Church, a miraculous phenomenon took place which was directly experienced and verified by the Vatican Congregation of Rites itself (presently known as the Congregation for Divine Worship and the Discipline of the Sacraments).

Bishop de Caesare, of the Nola Diocese, had begun to send out small quantities of dust from the bones of the relics of Philomena to neighboring parishes and dioceses. It soon became evident to the bishop, however, that even though he continued to send out bone dust the amount of dust remaining never decreased—it seemed as if a miraculous multiplication of the dust was taking place.

When this apparent miracle was brought to the attention of the Congregation of Rites at the Vatican, they decided to conduct an experiment. The Congregation began to distribute the bone dust of Philomena to diverse parts of Italy, while at the same time sending out bone dust from the remains of another Roman martyr in the same manner. What the Congregation witnessed was a decrease in the amount of bone dust from the other Roman martyr's remains, but a miraculous preservation of the bone dust of Philomena, which did not diminish. The Holy See experienced first-hand the manifest will of God to make this young martyr known publicly through her historically documented miracles.[5]

The most famous miracle of Philomena, one directly confirmed by Pope Gregory XVI, was experienced by Venerable Pauline Jaricot, the daughter of a French aristocratic family, and a close friend of St. John Vianney.

Pauline was a tireless worker for the Church. She was the lay founder of the Vatican congregation *Propaganda Fide*, or the Society for the Propagation of the Faith. As a young woman she had gone to the textile workers of Lyon, to ask them to contribute a penny a week for the spread of the faith in missionary lands. This work became so successful that it eventually led to the Vatican taking over the guidance of the Society and developing it into a curial office of the Holy See under the title of *Propaganda Fide*. Venerable Pauline was also the founder of the Society of the Living Rosary.

In 1834, at the age of 35, Pauline Jaricot became gravely ill. She was dying of serious heart disease and it was thought she had only weeks left to live. At the encouragement of St. John

Vianney, she decided to undertake a pilgrimage to the tomb of St. Philomena—against all medical counsel.

Arriving in Rome en route to Mugnano, which was farther south, she stopped to visit with Gregory XVI, but being too ill she was unable to attend the scheduled audience. Out of respect for Pauline, the Holy Father went to see her personally at the Sacred Heart Convent where she was staying. Upon seeing her, Pope Gregory knew that she had not long to live, and asked her: "Pray for the Church as soon as you arrive in Paradise."

Pauline responded: "Yes, Holy Father, I promise you, but if I walk on foot to the Vatican upon my return from Mugnano, would your Holiness deign to proceed without delay to the final inquiry into the cause of Philomena?"

Gregory XVI replied, "Of course, for in that case it would be a first class miracle." But he personally had no doubt that Pauline's time on earth was at an end. Turning to the Italian Sister who had accompanied him on his visit, he said in Italian (so as not to be overheard by Pauline), "we will never see her again."

On August 8, 1835, Pauline arrived in Mugnano looking "more like a corpse than a living person," according to witnesses. By this time, Pauline was no longer able to speak.

That evening, the infirm woman attended a long ceremony at the church, but there was no miracle. On August 9, she attended several Masses, and received Holy Communion, and still there was no miracle. Pauline returned to the church on Sunday night, and again on Monday morning, August 10—still, no miracle.

By this time, the entire town of Mugnano was well aware of the drama taking place at the shrine of their little martyr. As the days passed and Pauline was not cured, the townspeople became increasingly worried, and adopted a good-hearted, but perhaps peculiarly southern Italian form of petition to St. Philomena: pounding on her grave, they reminded her that her reputation was at stake: "Do you hear us, Philomena? If you do not cure this pious lady, we will pray to you no more! We will have nothing to do with you! Return her to health right now!"

Later that day, on Monday the 10th—precisely at the moment of benediction of the Eucharistic Jesus, and 30 years to the day that Philomena arrived in Mugnano—Pauline Jaricot was completely and instantaneously cured.

The next day, before a huge crowd, Pauline set off walking without assistance towards Rome, and the crowds accompanied her much of the way. On her arrival in Rome, Pauline decided to visit the Holy Father unannounced. Upon entering the audience chamber, she shocked Gregory XVI, who immediately exclaimed: "Is it really you or an apparition of you? Is this really my dear daughter? And has she come back from the grave, or has God manifested in her favor the power of the Virgin-Martyr?"[6]

Stunned, Pope Gregory had Pauline walk throughout the halls of the Vatican repeatedly, and also requested her to stay in Rome for an entire year to verify her miraculous cure.

Keeping his word to Pauline, Pope Gregory XVI, on January 13, 1837, in a solemn decree *based solely on power of her undeniable miracles*, raised an unknown thirteen-year-old early martyr named Philomena to the altar of the Church, granting a Mass in her honor, and thereby giving official approval to public devotion to her. This liturgical honor constituted the only instance of a Proper Office being granted to a saint from the catacombs of whom nothing is known except her name and the bare fact that she was martyred for the Faith. "Filumena" was now officially *St. Philomena*, a canonized saint of the Catholic Church.

We must particularly underscore here the inspired wisdom of Pope Gregory XVI. The Holy Father rightly recognized the evidence of the large number of ecclesiastically documented miracles as being of greater importance than the secondary details of St. Philomena's personal history. God's manifested testimony to the historical reality of the person of St. Philomena through her supernatural intercession took precedence over the specific historical details of the virgin-martyr's earthly life. In effect, the Pope acknowledged the miracles in themselves *as historical facts*.

Authentic miracles constitute God's greatest confirmation of the historical reality of the human person in question, and, moreover, manifest heaven's desire for that person to be recognized and venerated by the People of God on earth. The miracles of St. Philomena assured Pope Gregory, and assure us, of her pre-eminent sanctity and her ongoing role in the life of the Church.

Typically, without documented miracles the cause of an individual person does not advance past the status of Servant of God, even with extensive evidence of an earthly life of heroic virtue. The Church places its greatest criteria for canonization, along with an essential testimony to the person's virtues, upon heaven's witness to the sanctity of the candidate which is made manifest through miracles obtained through the candidate's intercession.

It was therefore most appropriate for Gregory XVI to place greater importance upon the history of documented miracles through St. Philomena's intercession during the canonization discernment process, rather than upon the lack of personal details regarding St. Philomena's earthly existence. Beyond establishing the fact of her martyrdom, as the guidelines of the Church indicate should be done, it was, above all, the miracles of St. Philomena that moved the Church to proclaim her a saint. Similarly, contemporary examination of St. Philomena's status should use the same criterion of evaluation.

Notes

[1]   Cf. Msgr. Francis Trochu, La "petite sainte" du Curé d'Ars, Sainte Philomène, vierge et martyre, Librairie Catholique Emmanuel Vitte, Paris, 1929, as found in Magnificat, August, 1998, p. 139.

[2]   Cf. Fr. Francesco di Lucia, Relazione Istorica della Traslazione del Sacro Corpo di Santa Filomena, Vergine e Martire, da Roma a Mugnano del Cardinale, Naples, 1829, pp. 48-49, as found in Sr. Marie Helene Mohr, S.C., Saint Philomena, Powerful with God, Tan, 1988, p. 35.

[3]   Cf. Documentation from the Parish Shrine of Mugnano, commencing with di Lucia, Relazione, Vol. I, p. 1, and continuing with the Rector of Our Lady of Grace Church, Msgr. Gennaro Ippolito, Memorie e culto di santo Filomena Vergine e martire, Mormile, Naples, 1870, Ch. 25; also pp. 23-24, 256, 277, 42-48.

[4]   Cf. Fr. Gabriel Bouffier, S.J., La Vènèrable Servante de Dieu, Anna-Maria Taigi, Retaux, Paris, pp. 125-126, from Trochu, La "petite sainte," as found in Magnificat, August, 1998, pp. 142-143.

[5]   Presentation of the dossier of Bishop Basilici to the Sacred Congregation of Rites, June 17, 1835, presided over by Cardinal Galiffi, Vice-Prefect of the Congregation. Cf. also Msgr. François Trochu, La "petite sainte" du Curé d'Ars, Sainte Philomène, vierge et martyre, Librairie Catholique Emmanuel Vitte, Paris, 1929, p. 122.

[6]   Cf. Ippolito, Memorie, pp. 243, 55; Msgr. Deschamps du Manoir, Mugnano et sainte Philomène, p. 40; E. Sainte-Marie Perrin, Pauline Jaricot, fondatrice de la Société pour la Propagation de la Foi, 1799-1862, J. de Gigord, Paris, pp. 150-169, from Trochu, La "petite sainte," as found in Magnificat, August, 1998, p. 151.

CHAPTER II

PERSONAL HISTORY OF ST. PHILOMENA IN PRIVATE REVELATION

During that remarkable period of the 1830s, when miracles abounded through St. Philomena's intercession and the Church granted her public liturgical veneration,[1] three separate individuals in different parts of Italy (completely unknown to each other), began receiving details of the historical background of St. Philomena through various modes of private revelation. The most significant were locutions received by Sr. Luisa di Gesu in August of 1833, revelations which received approval by the Holy Office, (presently the Congregation for the Doctrine of the Faith) on December 21, 1833.

One day, while praying to St. Philomena, Sr. Luisa of Jesus thought she heard words coming from a statue of the saint giving her specific date of death, August 10, and details of her journey to Mugnano which were unknown to the general public.

Sr. Luisa, fearing she was suffering a delusion, increased her prayers and fasting, and, under obedience, observed complete silence during subsequent revelations.

Sr. Luisa's Superior then wrote to Fr. di Lucia, reporting the supposedly revealed details given about the Rome-Mugnano journey and asking about their veracity. Fr. di Lucia confirmed every detail of the revelation as perfectly accurate, and requested that the nun "be open" to any more revelations pertaining to the life of Philomena.

Under obedience, Sr. Luisa prayed for further information, and immediately the "same voice" began revealing the third to fourth century historical life of St. Philomena, which we here reproduce from the original text:

> My dear Sister, I am the daughter of a Prince who governed a small state in Greece. My mother is also of royal blood. My parents were without children. They were idolaters. They continually offered sacrifices and prayers to their false gods.
>
> A doctor from Rome named Publius lived in the palace in the service of my father. This doctor professed Christianity. Seeing the affliction of my parents, by the impulse of the Holy Spirit, he spoke to them of Christianity, and promised to pray for them if they consented to receive Baptism. The grace which accompanied his words enlightened their understanding and triumphed over their will. They became Christians and obtained the long desired happiness that Publius had assured them as the reward of their conversion. At the moment of my birth, they gave me the name of "Lumena," an allusion to the light of Faith of which I had been, as it were, the fruit. The day of my Baptism they called me "Filumena," or "Daughter of Light," because on that day I was born to the Faith. The affection which my parents bore me was so great that they had me always with them.
>
> It was on this account that they took me to Rome on a journey that my father was obliged to make on the occasion of an unjust war

with which he was threatened by the haughty Diocletian. I was then thirteen years old. On our arrival in the capital of the world, we proceeded to the palace of the Emperor and were admitted for an audience. As soon as Diocletian saw me, his eyes were fixed upon me. He appeared to be pre-possessed in this manner during the entire time that my father was stating with animated feelings everything that could serve for his defense.

As soon as Father had ceased to speak, the Emperor desired him to be disturbed no longer, to banish all fear, to think only of living in happiness. These are the Emperor's words, "I shall place at your disposal all the force of the Empire. I ask only one thing, that is the hand of your daughter." My father, dazzled with an honor he was far from expecting, willingly acceded on the spot to the proposal of the Emperor.

When we returned to our own dwelling, Father and Mother did all they could to induce me to yield to Diocletian's wishes and theirs. I cried, "Do you wish, that for the love of a man, I should break the promise I have made to Jesus Christ? My virginity belongs to him. I can no longer dispose of it." "But you were young then, too young," answered my father, "to have formed such an engagement." He joined the most terrible threats to the command that he gave me to accept the hand of Diocletian. The grace of my God rendered me invincible, and my father, not being able to make the Emperor relent, in order to disengage himself from the promise he had given, was obliged by Diocletian to bring me to the Imperial Chamber.

I had to withstand for some time beforehand a new attack from my father's anger. My mother, uniting her efforts to his, endeavored to conquer my resolution. Caresses, threats, everything was employed to reduce me to compliance. At last, I saw both of my parents fall at my knees and say to me with tears in their eyes, "My child have pity on your father, your mother, your country, our country, our subjects." "No! No," I answered them. "My virginity, which I have vowed to God, comes before everything, before you, before my country. My kingdom is heaven."

My words plunged them into despair and they brought me before the Emperor, who on his part did all in his power to win me. But his promises, his allurements, his threats, were equally useless. He then flew into a violent fit of anger and, influenced by the Devil, had me cast into one of the prisons of the palace, where he had me loaded with chains. Thinking that pain and shame would weaken the courage with which my Divine Spouse inspired me, he came to see me every day. After several days, the Emperor issued an order for my chains to be loosed, that I might take a small portion of bread and water. He renewed his attacks, some of which would have been fatal to purity had it not been for the grace of God.

The defeats which he always experienced were for me the preludes to new tortures. Prayer supported me. I did not cease to recommend myself to Jesus and his most pure Mother. My captivity had lasted thirty-seven days, when, in the midst of a heavenly light, I saw Mary holding the Divine Son in her arms. "My daughter," she said to me, "three days more of prison and after forty days you shall leave this state of pain." Such happy news made my heart beat with joy, but as the Queen of Angels had added that I should quit my prison, to sustain, in frightful torments a combat far more terrible than those preceding, I fell instantly from joy to the most cruel anguish; I thought it would kill me. "Have courage, my child," Mary then said to me; "are you unaware of the love of predilection that I bear for you? The name, which you received in baptism, is the pledge of it for the resemblance which it has to that of my Son and to mine. You are called Lumena, as your Spouse is called Light, Star, Sun, as I myself am called Aurora, Star, the Moon in the fullness of its brightness, and Sun. Fear not, I will aid you. Now nature, whose weakness humbles you, asserts its law. In the moment of combat, grace will come to lend you its force, and your Angel, who was also mine, Gabriel, whose name expresses strength, will come to your aid. I will recommend you especially to his care, as the well beloved among my children." These words of the Queen of Virgins gave me courage again, and the vision disappeared, leaving my prison filled with a celestial perfume. I experienced a joy out of this world. Something indefinable.

What the Queen of Angels had prepared me for was soon experienced. Diocletian, despairing of bending me, decided on public chastisement to offend my virtue. He condemned me to be stripped and scourged like the Spouse I preferred to him. These are his horrifying words: "Since she is not ashamed to prefer to an Emperor like me, a malefactor condemned to an infamous death by his own people, she deserves that my justice shall treat her as he was treated." The prison guards hesitated to unclothe me entirely but they did tie me to a column in the presence of the great men of the court. They lashed me with violence until I was bathed in blood. My whole body felt like one open wound, but I did not faint.

The tyrant had me dragged back to the dungeon, expecting me to die. I hoped to join my heavenly Spouse. Two angels, shining with light, appeared to me in the darkness. They poured a soothing balm on my wounds, bestowing on me a vigor I did not have before the torture.

When the Emperor was informed of the change that had come over me, he had me brought before him. He viewed me with a greedy desire and tried to persuade me that I owed my healing and regained vigor to Jupiter, another god, that he, the Emperor, had sent to me. He attempted to impress me with his belief that Jupiter desired me to be Empress of Rome. Joining to these seductive words promises of great honor, including the most flattering words, Diocletian tried to caress me. Fiendishly, he attempted to complete the work of Hell which he had begun. The Divine Spirit to whom I am indebted for constancy in preserving my purity seemed to fill me with light and knowledge, and to all the proofs which I gave of the solidity of our Faith, neither Diocletian or his courtiers could find an answer.

Then, the frenzied Emperor dashed at me, commanding a guard to chain an anchor around my neck and bury me deep in the waters of the Tiber. The order was executed. I was cast into the water, but God sent me two angels who unfastened the anchor. It fell into the river mud, where it remains no doubt to the present time. The angels transported me gently in full view of the multitude upon the riverbank. I came back unharmed, not even wet, after being plunged with the heavy anchor.

When a cry of joy rose from the debauchers on the shore, and so many embraced Christianity by proclaiming their belief in my God, Diocletian attributed my preservation to secret magic. Then the Emperor had me dragged through the streets of Rome and shot with a shower of arrows. My blood flowed, but I did not faint. Diocletian thought that I was dying and commanded the guards to carry me back to the dungeon. Heaven honored me with a new favor there. I fell into a sweet sleep, and I found myself, on awaking, perfectly cured.

Diocletian learned about it. "Well, then," he cried in a fit of rage, "let her be pierced with sharp darts a second time, and let her die in that torture." They hastened to obey him. Again, the archers bent their bows. They gathered all their strength, but the arrows refused to second their intentions. The Emperor was present. In a rage, he called me a magician, and thinking that the action of fire could destroy the enchantment, ordered the darts to be made red in a furnace and directed against my heart. He was obeyed, but these darts, after having passed through a part of the space which they were to cross to come to me, took a quite contrary direction and returned to strike those by whom they had been hurled. Six of the archers were killed by them. Several among them renounced paganism, and the people

began to render public testimony to the power of
God that protected me.

These murmurs and acclamations infuriated
the tyrant. He determined to hasten my death
by ordering my head to be cut off. My soul took
flight towards my heavenly spouse, who placed
me, with the crown of virginity and the palm of
martyrdom, in a distinguished place among the
elect. The day that was so happy for me and saw
me enter into glory was Friday, the third hour
after mid-day, the same hour that saw my Divine
Master expire.

There are several things noteworthy about this extraordinary
account. Historically, the evil Emperor Diocletian was indeed
known for executing Christians by arrows. Diocletian was also
known for killing Christians by tying anchors around their
necks and having them thrown into the Tiber. Furthermore,
Philomena being first named "Lumena," which means "light,"
and then being given her second name "Filumena" in baptism,
would be consistent with the way her name was depicted on
the tiles: "Lumena" first, and then combined with the last tile,
"Filumena."

Why is St. Philomena making such a powerful spiritual return
in our own times? I believe one reason is that the youth of today
need an example of heroic Christian purity, even when they do
not find support for purity from their society, their friends, nor
even at times from their own parents. Many of today's youth are
being exposed to numerous occasions of blasphemy and impurity
through pornography, immodest clothing, obscene movies, and
oftentimes, most tragically, with the consent of their parents.

Today's youth need a young heroic witness for the upholding
of Christian purity even if their peers and their own parents are
not encouraging them. They face situations very similar to those
which Philomena had to contend with. Both the Emperor and

her parents encouraged her to become the Empress of Rome—the highest position of power and fame the world could offer any woman. Similarly, our young people are continually tempted by the allure of power and pride and illicit pleasures. Because Philomena said yes to Christ and to his kingdom, it is little wonder that Jesus is making her well known again as the Patroness of Purity, for the young people of the twenty-first century.

The Popes of the Nineteenth and Twentieth Centuries

The Holy Fathers of the nineteenth and early twentieth century manifested remarkable devotion to the young Princess Virgin-Martyr. For example:

Pope Leo XII granted permission for altars to be dedicated and chapels to be erected in her honor, calling her the "Great Saint."[2] Pope Gregory XVI called St. Philomena the "Thaumaturga," the "wonder-worker" of the nineteenth century, and, as already mentioned, in 1837 he raised her to the "altar of the Church" with public devotion. He granted her a special feast (August 11) and also approved a Mass in her honor.[3]

Blessed Pope Pius IX had an exemplary devotion to St. Philomena. While still a bishop, he went on pilgrimage several times to her tomb to offer Mass, and as Pope, he declared St. Philomena the "Patroness of the Children of Mary."[4]

On Nov. 7, 1849, at a critical moment of his pontificate, Pius IX went on pilgrimage to the tomb of St. Philomena to seek her intercession at a time of Church crisis. A political revolution had taken place in Rome, and with a heavy heart Pius IX was obliged to leave the city. Joined by many young men of the region, the exiled Pontiff walked with olive and palm branches in hand to the tomb of St. Philomena to offer the Holy Sacrifice of the Mass and implore her intercession for an expedient return to Rome. While at the tomb, the Pope took the reliquary containing the vial of St. Philomena's dried blood, which had been found in her tomb, and traced the sign of the cross on his forehead. He was later to confide that when kneeling in prayer before the bones of St. Philomena, he received an interior certainty that he would soon return to Rome. Within a time much more brief than expected, Pius IX returned to the Vatican. In thanksgiving for this great grace received through St. Philomena, Bl. Pius IX granted upon her feast day a Proper Office and Mass specific to her, beyond the normal common office for virgins and martyrs. This was an honor never bestowed on any other Roman martyr who lacked an historical record.

At the moment of his death, Pius IX, with love and thanksgiving to the great saint, had his pectoral cross sent to rest on the altar holding the image of his special young intercessor.

Pope Leo XIII was another pope in the list of pontiffs who had a special love for St. Philomena. He also had a strong devotion to her before becoming Vicar of Christ. It was Leo XIII who commissioned the beginning of the Archconfraternity of St. Philomena, and it was he who with an almost unprecedented generosity approved and granted an indulgence to the wearing of the "Cord of St. Philomena."[5] This cord, which we will discuss in more detail later, was colored white and red in honor of the virginity and martyrdom of St. Philomena, and was strongly promoted by St. John Vianney (to whom most historians attribute the origins of the Cord). Not only did Leo XIII grant a plenary indulgence for those who wore the cord for the first time, but he also granted a plenary indulgence for three liturgical times of the year associated with St. Philomena. Furthermore, a plenary indulgence was granted to those wearing of the Cord at the hour of their death.[6]

In the twentieth century, Pope St. Pius X continued the strong papal tradition of veneration of St. Philomena. In 1905, on the occasion of the centenary of her arrival in Mugnano, he sent his gold ring to adorn the image of St. Philomena located over her tomb. In that same year, he beatified the Curé of Ars, St. John Vianney, who had such a primordial devotion to St. Philomena.

St. Pius X was also a great advocate of wearing the Cord of St. Philomena and declared, "all the decisions and declarations of his predecessors regarding St. Philomena should in no way be altered."[7] With this act he perpetuated devotion to St. Philomena for all times. Pius X also elevated the Archconfraternity of St. Philomena to the status of a universal archconfraternity.[8]

In sum, nineteen acts of the Holy See during the pontificates of five popes were issued in positive promotion of popular devotion to St. Philomena, in the forms of public liturgical veneration, archconfraternities, and plenary and partial indulgences. This succession of papal veneration and indulgences is arguably unprecedented in the pontifical granting of devotional privileges for any modern saint.

Notes

1   Cf. Solemn decree of Pope Gregory XVI, January 13, 1837, in papal approval of the rescript of the Sacred Congregation of Rites of September 6, 1834. Cf. Ippolito, *Memorie*, pp.122-123; Trochu, La *"petite sainte,"* p. 129.

2   Cf. Francesco di Lucia, *The Life and Miracles of Saint Philomena, Virgin and Martyr*, New York, O'Shea & Co., 1865, p. ix, as found in Mohr, *Saint Philomena*, p. 65.

3   Cf. Solemn decree of Pope Gregory XVI, January 13, 1837. Cf. Ippolito, *Memorie*, pp.122-123; Trochu, La *"petite sainte,"* p. 129.

4   Cf. Mohr, *Saint Philomena*, p. 68.

5   Cf. Pope Leo XIII, papal approbation of the Cord of St. Philomena and indulgences, December 15, 1883.

6   *Ibid.*

7   Cf. Pope St. Pius X, Apostolic Brief, *Pias Fidelium Societates*, May 21, 1912.

8   *Ibid.*

CHAPTER III

THE CURÉ AND HIS "DEAR LITTLE SAINT"

We have already mentioned the devotion to St. Philomena of such great souls in the Church as Bl. Anna Maria Taigi and Ven. Pauline Jaricot. Yet they are far from being the only saints who loved and honored her.

St. Peter Julian Eymard was cured of a serious illness after visiting St. John Vianney and being instructed by him to pray a novena to St. Philomena.[1] St. Peter Chanel, the first saint and martyr of Oceania, preached on St. Philomena and said that it was she, after Our Lady, who was his principal intercessor in his apostolate. He referred to St. Philomena as his "auxiliary."[2] Bl. Damien de Veuster of Molokai, the "Leper-Priest," dedicated his first parish church and first home to St. Philomena.[3] St. Madeleine Sophie Barat consistently invoked Philomena during difficulties in the establishment of her societies, and attributed a miraculous cure of a dying novice to her intercession.[4] Other devotees of St. Philomena from the ranks of the saints and blessed include St. Magdalene of Canossa, Bl. Bartolo Longo and Bl. Annibale Da Messina.

St. John Vianney and St. Philomena

There is little doubt, however, that the special relationship between St. John Vianney and St. Philomena, his "dear little saint," was beyond that of all other saints. From the first time he heard of St. Philomena, this old French priest and the young Roman martyr obtained a "union of heart" which led to consistent, direct, supernatural fruits and experiences. In fact, the Curé of Ars habitually attributed all miracles that came through him to the intercession of St. Philomena.

In 1837, the Curé of Ars erected the first chapel in France dedicated to his "dear little saint." This phenomenal combination of St. Philomena, "miracle worker of the nineteenth century," and St. John Vianney, reader of souls and now the universal patron saint of parish priests, produced wonders of grace awesome to behold.

Whenever someone would come to the Curé for healing or other graces, he would invariably direct them to St. Philomena with sure confidence, usually advising them to make a novena of prayer to her, visit her chapel, and commend their need to her with confidence. To those in need who could not come in person, St. John would send oil from lamps burning at her tomb in Mugnano.

As time progressed and the Curé's fame spread, thousands, and then tens of thousands of pilgrims came to Ars each year from all over the world. As many as 14 miracles per week were recorded in the parish chronicles. So many pilgrims came to Ars that an overwhelmed John Vianney once remarked in Catechism class: "Couldn't she work miracles somewhere else?" On one occasion a man from another part of France asked the Curé what sort of extraordinary things were occurring in the parish. He replied, "What do you mean, extraordinary things in my parish; you must not believe everything you hear." The man replied, "Well then, Father, when I get back... I will say nothing is happening in your parish." St. John was forced to admit, "In that case, you would be lying. You must not do that. Tell them that everything is happening through the intercession of the Blessed Virgin and St. Philomena. The deaf, the dumb, the blind, the paralyzed, and the possessed are healed. But it is only through the intercession of the Blessed Virgin and St. Philomena."

St. Philomena appeared to the Curé of Ars numerous times, including in May, 1843. Critically ill with double pneumonia, Fr. Vianney had been given up for dead. After receiving the last rites, he asked that Mass be offered for St. Philomena on his behalf. Immediately, St. Philomena appeared to the dying priest and healed him, and in the process revealed personal information to the Curé.[5]

This illumination led St. John to consult with St. Philomena about important decisions for the rest of his life.[6]

On another occasion, Vianney confided to a dear friend his account of an apparition of St. Philomena:

> I had a hard time discovering the will of God concerning an enterprise that bothered me. I asked to know the will of God. St. Philomena appeared to me; she had come down from heaven and she was beautiful, luminous, surrounded by a white cloud. She told me twice, "Your works are more perfect, because there is nothing more precious than the salvation of souls."[7]

The specific item troubling Vianney concerned a new church in Ars. The structure needed funding and the assistant pastor wished to take the money designated for the parish mission and use it for the new church. St. John did not feel peaceful about this transference of funds, and he therefore consulted St. Philomena. She instructed him to do what he originally planned to do, that is, to use the funds for the parish mission, because this work was "more perfect."[8]

While we cannot here provide an exhaustive survey of the hundreds of miracles that took place in Ars through St. Philomena and St. John Vianney, a few examples can illustrate the abundance of graces poured out through their combined intercession.

François Pertinand, a hotel-keeper at Ars, related this miracle during the canonization process of St. John Vianney:

> This is what happened to me. I came down with a serious illness which caused terrible swelling, to the point that it had reached my chest. I was taken to Villefranche for medical care. The doctors declared that my blood was contaminated and there was no remedy for it. With that, my parents absolutely wanted to take me back home. The Curé came to see me. He told me that I had only two days to live, but that if I were willing to have confidence and follow his advice, I would be healed. "If you make a novena to St. Philomena with your parents and me," he said, "when it is over you will go to Fourviere in thanksgiving." This seemed impossible to me, but I followed his advice anyway. On the fourth day I was able to get up; and on the ninth, I harnessed my horse myself and went to Lyons with my family.[9]

During the Curé's canonization process, Mrs. Marie Robert of Clermont-Ferrand relates the following incident, which occurred in September 1857:

> Father Vianney was teaching his eleven o'clock catechism class. I can still see him in his little stall next to the Blessed Virgin's altar. The omnibus arrived. All of a sudden the church door opened abruptly, causing us to turn our heads to look.

Three people were there by the holy water font: a woman, and a man holding a child in his arms. Looking at these newcomers, Father Vianney said to them with a sigh, "Poor people! You came so far to seek something here that you have at home! Your faith is great!" Then he went on with his catechism lesson.

At the end, after reciting the Angelus, he spoke again to the father and mother in a loud voice, saying, "Take your child to St. Philomena, over there to the left!" The unfortunates crossed the church and went to kneel before the statue of St. Philomena. Suddenly we heard a loud noise of moving chairs: the father had passed out on hearing his son speak for the first time. The six-year-old boy had been paralyzed, deaf and dumb from birth. "Nice Papa, nice!" the child said in his native patois, and he began to walk. The man explained to us, weeping with joy, "We came to Ars to ask for the healing of our son, who has never talked and never walked."[10]

Mrs. Claudine Raymond, from Chalonsur-Saone, was suffering a great deal from a chronic infection of the larynx and bronchial tubes. She could not speak the slightest word without feeling a pain in her throat which was described as "being burned with a red-hot iron." She communicated with those around her by writing on a slate. Finally, abandoned by the doctors, she had recourse to Father Vianney. The following is the woman's account as testified during the canonization process:

> I consulted with him on my condition. He said to me, "My child, the remedies of earth are useless for you; you have already had too many of them administered to you. But God wants to heal you.

Speak to St. Philomena. Place your slate on her altar. Do violence to her. Tell her that if she does not want to give you your voice back, she will give you hers!"

At once I went and cast myself at the feet of the little Saint; I was healed as soon as I had said my prayer. I had not spoken for two years and had been suffering acutely for six. When I returned to Madame Favier's where I was lodging, I read a few pages on confidence in the Blessed Virgin in a loud voice in front of several People. I was truly cured.

When I saw Father Vianney again, he said to me, "My child, do not forget to make your thanksgiving, and make sure you are here for the feast of St. Philomena." I was faithful to his recommendation. During Mass on the following August 11, I sang a hymn in honor of my dear benefactress in a loud, sustained voice. After the office, Father Vianney congratulated me for having obtained from the St. Philomena the faculty of singing as well as that of speaking.[11]

The profound unity of heart which manifested itself in these ecclesiastically documented miracles makes one thing unquestionably clear: *St. Philomena is a real person in the Communion of Saints* and an active presence in the Church on Earth. How could any question remain as to the true historical existence of St. Philomena, or concerning her saintly existence in heaven, when another canonized saint of the stature of St. John Vianney has perpetually testified to her reality, a reality guaranteed by intercession, miracles, and even by actual apparitions of the young saint? Either St. John Vianney was a great saint or he was gravely psychologically disturbed. If he was insane, the Church would not have canonized him, as his mystical and supernatural experiences, especially with St. Philomena, were so much a part of his entire priestly life and spirituality. If he was sane, then we must admit that St. Philomena exists, as the Curé assures us she does.

Indeed, the Curé of Ars once declared "I have never asked for anything through the intercession of my little saint without having been answered." This heavenly union of hearts between St. Philomena and St. John Vianney, which led to so many graces being granted the Mystical Body of Christ, is beautifully conveyed in the words of the late Henry Cardinal Manning of England:

> Mysterious and wonderful is the sympathy which thrills through the communion of saints, unbroken by distance, undimmed by time, unchilled by death! The youthful saint went forth from her mother's arms to die for Christ; the lictor's ax cropped the budding lily, and pious hands gathered it up and laid it in the tomb; and so fifteen centuries went by, and none on earth thought upon the virgin martyr who was following the Lamb withersoever He went, till the time came when the Lord would have her glory to appear; and then He chose a champion for her in the lonely toil worn priest to whom he had given a heart as childlike, and a love as heroic as her own; he gave her to be the helpmate of his labors, and bade her stand by him to shelter his humility behind the brightness of her glory lest he should be affrighted at the knowledge of his own power with God.[12]

Notes

1   Cf. relation by the Superior General of the Blessed Sacrament Sisters, *Messager de Sainte Philomène*, January 1897, from Trochu, *La "petite sainte,"* as found in *Magnificat*, August, 1998, p. 161.

2   Cf. Trochu, *La "petite sainte,"* p. 216.

3   *Ibid.*, p. 217.

4   Cf. Geoffrey de Grandmaison, *La bienheureuse Mère Barat*, Gabalda, 1909, p. 198.

5   Cf. archives of the Parish of Ars and ecclesiastical records relative to the Process of Beatification and Canonization of John Vianney and attribution of miracles to St. Philomena, Process of the Ordinary and Apostolic Processes, e.g., *Procès de l'Ordinaire*, Aug. 12, 1864, II, p. 1447; *Procès apostolique ne pereant*, October 10, 1876, pp. 1215-1216. Cf. also Trochu, *La "petite sainte,"* as found in *Magnificat*, August, 1998, pp. 158, 167-168.

6   Cf. Trochu, *La "petite sainte,"* as found in *Magnificat*, August, 1998, pp. 158ff.

7   Baroness Alix de Belvey, *Procès de l'Ordinaire*, Vol. I, pp. 253-254, from Trochu, *La "petite sainte,"* as found in *Magnificat*, August, 1998, p. 158

8   *Ibid.*

9   François Pertinand, *Procès apostolique ne pereant*, p. 827, from Trochu, *La "petite sainte,"* as found in *Magnificat*, August, 1998, p. 163.

10   Archives of the Sanctuary at Ars.

11   Mrs. Claudine Raymond, *Procès de l'Ordinaire*, Vol. II, p. 1459, from Trochu, *La "petite sainte,"* as found in *Magnificat*, August, 1998, p. 165.

12   Di Lucia, *The Life and Miracles of Saint Philomena*, p. 12, as found in Mohr, *Saint Philomena*, pp. 62-63.

CHAPTER IV

PERIOD OF CONTROVERSY

The 1961 Declaration by the Sacred Congregation of Rites

After such an exceptional testimony by popes and saints alike to the reality and miraculous intercessory power of the thirteen-year-old early Christian martyr, one would have thought that the place of St. Philomena amongst the great saints of the Church would have been assured for all time. Nonetheless, trouble and controversy were ahead for devotion to the Princess-saint.

In 1961, a statement from the Congregation of Rites caused considerable surprise and misunderstanding. While engaged in a revision of the Church calendar, they removed many of the traditional feasts in honor of Jesus, Mary and various saints, including the feast of St. Philomena. Many wondered if in this calendar revision St. Philomena had been "de-sainted" by the Church.

It is important, first of all, to note that the 1961 instruction was only a "liturgical directive." It was not an ecclesial declaration that St. Philomena was no longer a saint. Nor did it prohibit the popular devotion to St. Philomena that has received repeated approbation by the Papal Magisterium. There was no suspension or prohibition of the Universal Archconfraternity of St. Philomena granted by St. Pius X. To this day public veneration of St. Philomena continues with the full approval of the Holy See and the diocese of Nola, in which the Mugnano shrine of St. Philomena is located.

Why was St. Philomena removed from the calendar? Ironically, the reason given was the supposed lack of historical evidence for the existence of Philomena, despite numerous documented miracles and the support of popes and saints. This argument against Philomena rested principally on the questionable conclusions of one early twentieth century archeologist, Oracio Marucchi. In 1903, he posited that the apparent mis-ordering of the 3 tiles on the grave alleged to be Philomena's—starting with "LUMENA" on first tile, instead of "PAXTE"—proved that the tiles had come from another, earlier, grave and had been re-used in hers. Therefore, he argued, the grave and remains discovered in 1802 were not that of "Filumena" but of another, unknown person.

Marucchi's claims have been comprehensively countered and overturned by many renowned European historians and archeologists. The Jesuit archeologist Guiseppe Bonavenia was one of the first to respond to Marucchi. In 1907 he reminded the archaeological world that it was a frequent custom in the catacombs to begin epigraphs on the second tile, beginning with "peace to you." Hence, when the Vatican's official Custodian of Holy Relics, Msgr. Ponzetti, read the inscription beginning from the second tile as "PAX TECUM FILUMENA," he read it correctly.

It was also very possible that the original maker of the tomb, finding himself unable to write the entire name of "Filumena" on the first tile, wrote the "FI" on the last tile and "LUMENA" on the first, allowing him to conserve artistic proportion. In any case, there were at least 12 graves in the Priscilla Catacombs that began with "PAX TECUM," "PAX TIBI," or "IN PACE." Marucchi's theory that the order of Philomena's tiles argued against the grave being hers was shown to be groundless.[1] Furthermore, the tiles used on Philomena's grave date at least from the third century, precluding them from being those of an earlier second-century grave, as Marucchi alleged. The early Christians did not re-use brick tiles, only marble, because marble was very expensive and brick was not, and those of Philomena's are of brick.

Two more contemporary archeologists, Prandi and Mustillo, after examining the actual tiles in 1963 also stated that the stance of Marucchi had no foundation. The evidence rested not only on tile position but on tile condition. The two archeologists pointed out that had the tiles been removed from another grave in order to be re-used for Philomena's, damage would have been done to the outer edges of the tile where previously cemented. However, no damage was found on the tiles from St. Philomena's loculus: "During the process of going from first to second usage, chips would have very likely been made to the edges of the brick tiles… [These tiles of Philomena] still have sound and undamaged matching edges along the line of fracture."[2]

Marucchi had never examined the gravesite nor the tiles themselves, but rather had made an abstract hypothesis without the necessary archeological investigation. Contemporary Austrian historian, George Markhof, strongly criticized Marucchi's conclusions: "I hold the judgment of the Italian archeologist Marucchi to be superficial… something extremely surprising considering the excellent renown he enjoyed. Evidently he was prejudiced against Saint Philomena, and not disposed, as is suitable for a scientist, to investigate the merits of this affair in an objective manner."[3]

The most recent studies in 2005 by Dr. Carlo Lalli, a scientist at the Institute delle Pietre Dure di Firenze, confirms that a) the vial found in the tomb does indeed contain blood, and even a small fragment of bone, something that had also been disputed; b) scientific examination of the three stones used to seal St. Philomena's tomb proved that they were sealed only once, and that they therefore belonged to the person whose bones were found within. Dr. Lalli's examination of the three tiles also resulted in another theory being advanced for the reason they appeared to be out of order: two of the three stones used to seal St. Philomena's tomb were originally only one stone that had been cut in two. This was done because the tomb needed three stones to correctly seal it. Unfortunately, after the mason had drawn the name and symbols of St. Philomena he realized that the tomb was wider on one end, thus necessitating a re-arrangement of the stones from the order he had initially planned on, so as to assure a proper fit. The end result was that the stones that sealed the tomb read "LUMENA PAXTE CUMFI" instead of "PAXTE CUMFI LUMENA."

On a pastoral and practical level, how should one respond to the 1961 directive? In an audience with Pope Paul VI, Bishop Sebastião Fernandes of Mysore, India, whose episcopal cathedral in Mysore was named after and dedicated to St. Philomena, asked that very question of the Holy Father. In a 1964 letter sent to the Mugnano Shrine by Bishop Fernandes, he testifies to the response given by the Paul VI:

> "What must I do for the people in my diocese who are greatly troubled by the decree of the Sacred Congregation regarding St. Philomena?" Paul VI responded, "Do not let it disturb you and do not disturb your people; let devotion to St. Philomena continue as before" ("proseguiva come prima").[4]

When the controversy first arose at the beginning of the twentieth century, Fr. Louis Petit, Director of the "Work of St. Philomena" in France, was received by Pope St. Pius X in a papal audience on June 6, 1907. During the audience, the Pope commented on the controversy, as documented by Fr. Petit immediately following the audience:

> I am very saddened by all that is being written about her. How can such things be possible?... How can they not see that the great argument in favor of devotion to St. Philomena is the Curé of Ars? Through her, in her name, by means of her intercession, he obtained countless graces,

continual wonders. His devotion to her was well known by everyone; he recommended her constantly...

We read the name, Filumena, on her tomb. Whether it be her own name or whether she has another, what does it matter? It remains, it is certain, that the soul which animated those sacred remains was a pure and holy soul that the Church has declared to be the soul of a virgin and martyr. That soul was so beloved by God, so pleasing to the Holy Spirit, that she has obtained the most wonderful graces for those who have had recourse to her intercession.[5]

When all is said and done, the name and historical details of the young virgin-martyr are not as important as the vast quantity of her miracles, Heaven's own testimony to her reality and sanctity. Her name and historical details are not as important as the truth that the person to whom the sacred remains found in the tomb belonged was declared a virgin and a martyr by the Church, and that she is so beloved by God that she has been granted the ability to intercede for us in an exceptional way.

These theological and historical facts should place the questionable, and secondary, archeological questions in their proper, subordinate place.

The 2001 Roman Martyrology

A more recent resurgence of the controversy took place with the 2001 publication of the revised Roman Martyrology by the Congregation of Worship and the Discipline of the Sacraments. The omission of St. Philomena was interpreted by various media sources to indicate that the Catholic Church no longer recognized her as a saint. This conclusion is inaccurate for several reasons.

St. Philomena had never been included in the Roman martyrologies in the first place, and therefore was not "removed."

The Roman Martyrology does not, and never did, constitute a comprehensive compilation of every saint and martyr recognized by the Church, and was never introduced by the Congregation of Worship and the Discipline of the Sacraments as such. Because a saint is not in the Martyrology does not mean the Church does not recognize that person as a saint.

The Holy See continues to permit public devotion to St. Philomena, which obviously pre-supposes the Church's continued belief in her existence. The universal shrine at Mugnano still operates with the blessing of the local Bishop of Nola, and the universal archconfraternity continues with ecclesiastical approval as well—and has experienced a significant worldwide renewal and promulgation of veneration to St. Philomena since the Second Vatican Council. It must also be kept in mind that historically the Papal Magisterium has granted many plenary and partial indulgences for devotion to her, supported and introduced liturgical veneration of St. Philomena, and granted universal approbation to her archconfraternity.[6]

Notes

[1]   Cf. the response to Marucchi by Guiseppe Bonavenia, in *Controversia sul celeberrimo epitaffio di Santa Filomena V. e M.*, Roma, Filiziani, (1906); and continued in *La questione puramente archeologica* (1907); cf. also the refutation of Marucchi's theory and the summation of several archeological contributions which offer refutations of the Marucchi theory in Trochu, *La "petite sainte,"* pp. 255-315. For more recent archeological studies countering the Marucchi theory, cf. Fr. Ferrua, S.J., *Archeological Study of the Bipedals of St. Philomena*, Archives of Mugnano Sanctuary; Prandi, Mustillo, and Guarducci, *Graffiti di S. Pietro*, I, Rome, November 29, 1963, p. 501; George Mauter Markhof, *Das unbequeme Wunder, kirchenstreit um Fhilomena*, Vienna, 1981.

[2]   Fr. Ferrua, S.J., *Report on the Epigraph: LUMENA-PAX TE-CUM FI*; Fr. Giovanni Braschi, *Santa Filomena (La Controversia de Filomena)*, 1985.

[3]   Markhof, *Das unbequeme Wunder*, as found in Braschi, *Santa Filomena*.

[4]   Mugnano Archives, 1964.

[5]   Rev. Louis Petit, *Messager de sainte Philomène*, July 1907, pp. 356-363; Trochu, *La "petite sainte,"* pp. 141-142.

[6]   Fr. Giovanni Braschi, Rector of the Mugnano shrine, has documented substantial and widespread increase in national and international pilgrimages to the shrine, the extent of which has necessitated major reconstruction at the shrine for the extended housing of pilgrims (completed September, 2002). Archconfraternity chapters have multiplied internationally, reaching all five continents, with accentuated increase coming from the British Isles (Ireland, Scotland, Great Britain), the Philippines, and the several locales within the United States; cf. Mugnano newsletters, e-mail dispatches, 2000-2002.

CHAPTER V

PRESENT PROCESS OF BEATIFICATION AND CANONIZATION

Neither the 1961 directive of the Congregation of Rites to remove St. Philomena from the calendar, nor her omission in the revised Roman Martyrology, negatively affect the papally established and ecclesiastically approved popular devotion to St. Philomena that continues with Church sanction in our own day. This is even further confirmed when we consider the Church's norms for beatification and canonization, and examine the case of St. Philomena in that light.

The Church's present process of beatification and canonization comprises the following stages: The heroic virtue or martyrdom of the individual being proposed for beatification/canonization is historically established; a miracle must be attributed to the direct intercession of the Servant of God for beatification, which then permits, by papal decree, public veneration in a particular, limited sphere of the Church (usually in the form of a Mass and office issued in honor of the blessed); another miracle must be attributed to the blessed, which occurred after the process of beatification, whereby public veneration is, by precept, extended to the universal Church by the pontiff.[1]

Beyond this process of formal canonization, there is also "equivalent canonization," where the formal canonical process has not been introduced, but the individual has received more than one hundred years of public cultus and their sanctity is recognized by the pope.[2]

If we apply these contemporary criteria for beatification and canonization to the case of St. Philomena, we find a rather definitive case for her present status as a canonized saint. The discovery of the blood vial and the palm branch symbol at her grave indicate Christian martyrdom, one of the two criteria for the first stage (which actually constitutes the highest form of heroic virtue). Great numbers of documented miracles took place at the Mugnano Shrine from 1805 to 1837, including the papally witnessed miraculous cure of Pauline Jaricot, which led to Gregory XVI's decree granting public liturgical cultus to the particular region of Nola (which is at least equivalent to the liturgical cultus granted to a "blessed"). A great quantity of miracles were recorded in Church proceedings, both in Mugnano and in Ars, France, which occurred during the period following the granting of particular public veneration.

Pope John Paul II reiterated, in his Apostolic Constitution implementing new norms for beatification and canonization, *Divinus Perfectionis Magister,* that either martyrdom or heroic virtue must be historically established for the process of beatification of a candidate, but not both. Therefore, a miracle is no longer required for the beatification of a martyr, as is still required for a non-martyred confessor of the faith.[3] Once martyrdom has been historically verified, the candidate can be immediately beatified without further evidence of a miracle or extended historical documentation of his life or heroic virtue. These revised norms would, in themselves, establish Philomena as a blessed solely in virtue of her martyrdom, with the certain fulfillment of the subsequent requirement of a documented miracle necessary for formal canonization.

Additionally in the case of Philomena, we have ample abundance of Church-recognized miracles, as well as the official act of Pope Gregory XVI raising her to the altars of the universal Church in 1837. This is a liturgical act proper only to a canonized saint. Gregory XVI, through this act, liturgically canonized Philomena, in an act of the ordinary Papal Magisterium which, guided by the Holy Spirit, should safeguard the perpetual status of Philomena as a saint.

Notes

1   John Paul II, Apostolic Constitution *Divinus Perfectionis Magister,* January 25, 1983; cf. also *Canonization Process,* Release of the Holy See Press Office, September 12, 1997.

2   Cf. T. Ortolan, *DTC,* 2.2: 1634-42; E. Dublanchy, *DTC,* 4.2:2186-87; Benedict XIV, *De servorum Dei beatificatione et beatorum canonizatione,* Vol. 4, (Prato, 1839-42); Green, *Canonization, NCE,* Vol. 3, p. 61.

3   John Paul II, *Divinus Perfectionis Magister,* 3; cf. also *Canonization Process,* Release of the Holy See Press Office, n. 5.

CHAPTER VI

MAJOR FORMS OF DEVOTION
TO ST. PHILOMENA

In light of the extraordinary history of miracles attributed to St. Philomena, and the fervent devotion paid to her by popes and saints alike, it is only to our good that we would respond to Heaven's manifestation of her supernatural power of intercession by our own personal "yes" to her—a love and devotion that allows us to benefit spiritually from her exceptional mediation. There are four principal forms of devotion to St. Philomena: the Cord of St. Philomena, the Oil of St. Philomena, the Chaplet of St. Philomena, and the Novena to St. Philomena.

The Cord of St. Philomena

The Cord of St. Philomena was a devotional practice strongly promoted by St. John Vianney (in fact, most believe that he originated it). The Cord is made of red and white wool, linen, or cotton, and is tied around the body. The colors red and white are in honor of the martyrdom and virginity of St. Philomena. At the end of Cord are two knots, again symbolizing virginity and martyrdom.

No ceremony is required in conferring or wearing the Cord, but the Cord must be blessed by a priest or deacon, using any standard form of the blessing of an object. The Cord is usually worn under one's clothing, and the faithful who wear it are encouraged to pray the following simple prayer daily: "O St. Philomena, virgin and martyr, pray for us that through your powerful intercession we may obtain that purity of mind and heart which leads to the perfect love of God. Amen."

On June 15, 1968, the Sacred Congregation of Rites issued the new *Enchiridion of Indulgences*, which suppressed all previous indulgences that are not included in the new enchiridion. Previously, the Holy See had granted the following plenary indulgences for wearing St. Philomena's Cord, some of which were at the expressed desire of the popes themselves: a plenary indulgence on the day the Cord is worn for the first time; on May 25, the anniversary of the discovery of her body; on August 11, feast of St. Philomena; on December 15, the anniversary of the approval of the cord; and, most remarkably, at the moment of an individual's death. Although the St. Philomena Cord indulgences are not included in the 1968 Enchiridion, the Cord, which should still be blessed by a priest, remains a powerful sacramental, and in light of its previous traditional papal recognition must certainly continue to be a powerful spiritual instrument in the contemporary battle for Christian faith and purity.

The Oil of St. Philomena

In 1805, within the first octave of St. Philomena's remains arriving in Mugnano, the mother of a blind child dipped her fingers into the oil that was burning in front of the altar of the saint. As soon as she anointed the eyelids of her blind child, the child was immediately cured. The oil coming from lamps burning perpetually at the tomb of St. Philomena continues to be a physical instrument of countless cures. These physical cures from St. Philomena Oil are reported to the Sanctuary of St. Philomena in Mugnano to this day, from all over world.

Recently during a U.S. radio program on St. Philomena, a mother called in and spoke of her child's repeated experience with "night terrors," the child waking in the middle of the night in full scream over terrifying nightmares. After the woman applied St. Philomena Oil to the child before putting him to bed, the night terrors immediately ceased, never to be repeated.

Oil from the tomb of St. Philomena is obtainable from the Sanctuary. The Oil can also be acquired from authorized St. Philomena Archconfraternity U.S. Distribution centers, but the Oil itself must come from the Sanctuary in Mugnano, which is burned next to Philomena's sacred remains.

The Chaplet of St. Philomena

This simple chaplet was composed by the Curé of Ars, and consists in the praying of the Creed, three Our Fathers in praise and glory to the three Persons of the Holy Trinity, thirteen Hail Marys in honor of the thirteen years of the life of the "princess-saint," or the following prayer as a substitute for the Hail Mary: "Hail, O Holy St. Philomena, my dear patroness. As my advocate with thy Divine Spouse, intercede for me now and at the hour of my death. St. Philomena, beloved daughter of Jesus and of Mary, pray for us who have recourse to thee. Amen." The Chaplet ends with the invocation: "Hail, O Illustrious St. Philomena, who so courageously shed thy blood for Christ, I bless the Lord for all the graces He has bestowed upon thee, during thy life, especially at thy death, I praise and glorify Him for the honor and power with which He has crowned thee, and I beg thee to obtain for me from God the graces I ask through thy intercession. Amen."

The Chaplet is a beautiful way of manifesting our daily love to St. Philomena, and is well-suited in its simplicity for family prayer by all members, young and old.

The Novena to St. Philomena

The fourth major devotion to St. Philomena is the nine-day novena to her, also strongly recommended by St. John Vianney.

Although there are several diverse nine-day novenas to St. Philomena, one popular version of the prayer prayed for nine days is as follows:

> O faithful virgin and glorious martyr, St. Philomena, who works so many miracles on behalf of the poor and sorrowing, have pity on me. Thou knowest the multitude and diversity of my needs. Behold me at thy feet, full of misery, but full of hope. I entreat thy charity, O great Saint! Graciously hear me and obtain from God a favorable answer to the request which I now humbly lay before thee … (Here specify your petition.) I am firmly convinced that through thy merits, through the scorn, the sufferings and the death thou didst endure, united to the merits of the Passion and death of Jesus, thy Spouse, I shall obtain what I ask thee, and in the joy of my heart I will bless God, who is admirable in His Saints. Amen.

The St. Philomena Novena is of course not limited to any particular category of intention, but has traditionally been especially efficacious for causes of purity and chastity, spiritual and physical healings for families (particularly children), and financial needs.

All items of devotion, cords, oil, novenas, prayers and literature can be obtained by directly contacting the Sanctuary of St. Philomena in Mugnano, Italy.

In conclusion, I would like to add my own personal testimony to this young saint of purity, and encourage you to open your homes and your hearts to St. Philomena.

Indeed, I can echo the words of St. Augustine, "Late have I loved Thee," in reference to St. Philomena. This "Little Sister of the Mystical Body" has come late into my life, but with tremendous power. Her presence in my spiritual life and that of my family has brought great graces to our marriage, new peace and grace of purity into our family life, a newly resolved commitment to Christian holiness, and striving for courage under persecution. My wife and I named our eighth child "Philumena" in thanksgiving for the many blessings the saint's spiritual friendship has bestowed on our family. We can testify to her great power with God and have experienced her almost tangible presence in our home. I invite you to welcome St. Philomena into your families, into your marriages, into your priestly and religious lives, into your hearts. Trust in her friendship. She and the Blessed Mother, who always accompanies her daughter, will not disappoint you.

St. Philomena, powerful with God, pray for us!

St. Philomena Shrine, Mugnano, Italy:

Santuario Santa Filomena
83027 Mugnano del Cardinale
Avellino
Italy
Tel: 011-39-081-825-7204
Fax: 011-39-081-511-2733
Email: SantaFilomena@philomena.it
Website: www.philomena.it

Litany of St. Philomena
(Composed by St. John Vianney, the Curé of Ars)

Lord, have mercy on us.
Lord, have mercy on us.
Lord, have mercy on us. Christ hear us.
Christ, graciously hear us.
God, the Father of Heaven,
have mercy on us.
God the Son, Redeemer of the world,
have mercy on us.
God the Holy Spirit,
have mercy on us.
Holy Trinity, one God.
have mercy on us.

Holy Mary, Queen of Virgins
pray for us. (repeat after each invocation)
St. Philomena,
St. Philomena, filled with abundant graces from your birth,
St. Philomena, faithful imitator of Mary,
St. Philomena, model of virginity,
St. Philomena, temple of perfect humility,
St. Philomena, inflamed with zeal for the glory of God,
St. Philomena, victim of love for Jesus,
St. Philomena, example of strength and perseverance,
St. Philomena, invincible champion of chastity,
St. Philomena, mirror of most heroic virtue,
St. Philomena, firm and intrepid in the face of torments,
St. Philomena, scourged like your Divine Spouse,
St. Philomena, pierced by a rain of arrows,
St. Philomena, consoled in chains by the Mother of God,
St. Philomena, miraculously healed in prison,
St. Philomena, comforted by the Angels in your torments,
St. Philomena, who preferred torments and the agonies of death
to the splendor of the throne,

St. Philomena, who converted witnesses by your martyrdom,
St. Philomena, who wore out the fury of your tormentors,
St. Philomena, protectress of the innocent,
St. Philomena, patroness of youth,
St. Philomena, refuge of the unfortunate,
St. Philomena, health of the sick and infirmed,
St. Philomena, new light of the Church Militant,
St. Philomena, who confounds the impiety of the world,
St. Philomena, who rejuvenates the faith and courage of the faithful,
St. Philomena, whose name is glorious in Heaven and feared in Hell,
St. Philomena, made illustrious by the most splendid miracles,
St. Philomena, powerful with God,
St. Philomena, who reigns in glory,

Lamb of God, You take away the sins of the world;
 spare us, O Lord.
Lamb of God, You take away the sins of the world;
 graciously hear us, O Lord.
Lamb of God, You take away the sins of the world;
 have mercy on us.

V. Pray for us, O Worker of Wonders, St. Philomena,
R. That we may be made worthy of the promises of Christ.

Let us pray.

O Lord, through the intercession of St. Philomena, Virgin and Martyr, whose eminent purity and practice of every virtue was most pleasing to you, pardon our sins and grant us the grace of _____ (add your special intention), through the same Christ, Our Lord. Amen.